Perfect your sight-rea

A workbook for examinations

Piano Grade 2

Paul Harris

NAME		
EXAMINATION RECORD		
Grade	**Date**	**Mark**

TEACHER'S NAME	
TELEPHONE	

© 2000 by Faber Music Ltd
First published in 2000 by Faber Music Ltd
3 Queen Square London WC1N 3AU
Music and text set by Silverfen Ltd
Cover illustration by Drew Hillier
Printed in England by Caligraving Ltd
All rights reserved

ISBN 0-571-52022-7

To buy Faber Music publications or to find out about the full range of titles available
please contact your local music retailer or Faber Music sales enquiries:

Faber Music Limited, Burnt Mill, Elizabeth Way
Harlow, CM20 2HX. England
Tel: +44 (0)1279 82 89 82   Fax: +44 (0)1279 82 89 83
Email: sales@fabermusic.com   www.fabermusic.com

FaberＦＦ MUSIC

INTRODUCTION

It is arguable that the ability to sight-read is perhaps the most essential aspect of musicianship for the majority of both developing and established musicians. It is not too far-fetched to suggest that young players able to read music with the same degree of fluency and accuracy as words, would present their teachers with a rather different kind of challenge. Instead of continually correcting mistakes, more time could be spent on things *musical!*

Sight-reading is dependent on co-ordinating a number of processes all at the same time; this is a technique that can be both taught and developed. The human brain is quite capable of dealing with many thoughts and actions simultaneously; it's not at all uncommon in the helter-skelter lives we lead in today's busy world, and we can all do it! It is the ability to concentrate – to focus your mind on a task – that we must develop if sight-reading is to become really fluent and secure.

Using the workbook

You can use this workbook as a follow-on to **Improve your sight-reading! – Piano Grade 2.**

After three introductory stages, each stage is set out virtually identically to those in *Improve your sight-reading! – Piano Grade 2.* The **rhythmic exercises** help to develop the ability to feel and maintain a steady beat: clap or tap the lower line (the beat) while singing the upper line to 'la'; tap the lower line with your foot and clap the upper line, or tap the lower line with one hand and the upper line with the other.

The **melodic exercises** have been carefully devised to help you recognise melodic shapes – such as scales and arpeggios – at first glance. These begin with special exercises, written in semibreves, to help with note recognition; play these as slowly as necessary, and in your own time, in order to identify and correctly locate each note.

The **prepared pieces with questions** are to help you think about and understand the pieces before you play them. Put your answers in the spaces provided.

Finally, your teacher will give you an **unprepared text** to read at sight. Make sure you have read the *Sight-reading Checklist* on page 24 before you begin each piece.

Your teacher will mark your work according to accuracy. With the exception of the introductory stages, each stage carries a maximum of 50 marks and your work will be assessed as follows:

2 marks for each of the six questions relating to the prepared piece (total 12).
18 marks for the prepared piece itself.
20 marks for the unprepared test. (Teachers can devise similar questions for the unprepared test, and take the answers into account when allocating a final mark.)

Space is given at the end of each stage for you to keep a running total of your marks as you progress. If you are scoring 40 or more each time you are doing well!

Don't forget to 'practise' the sight-reading pieces at home. Until a piece is really learned, there is still a strong element of sight-reading involved – even when the piece has been repeated a few times.

The really important factor is always to remember to concentrate – *feeling the pulse* and *thinking in the key.*

Take your sight-reading seriously – it will pay you great dividends.

The author wishes to thank Graeme Humphrey and Tuck May Loke for many helpful suggestions.

STAGE 1

In **Perfect your sight-reading! – Piano Grade 1** we learnt about the different things you have to think about when sight-reading a piece of music.

Here's the list again to refresh your memory:

- keeping a steady pulse
- reading notes correctly
- understanding rhythmic patterns and combining them with notes
- remembering the key signature (if there is one)
- looking ahead
- observing dynamic markings and other expression marks
- fingering

Apart from being able to play in more keys, the main difference between Grade 1 and Grade 2 is that you now have to read and play with both hands at the same time. It's not difficult! Try reading the following phrases. Look out – they read downwards!

Once	in	there	He	cloak	book	His	indeed!
upon	a	lived	wore	and	of	favourite	It's easy
a	land	a	a	owned	spells.	was	to
time	far away	wizard.	great	a		'Yes	sight-read!'

Reading words downwards may feel strange at first but it is really no more difficult than reading from left to right, and it is all that you have to be able to do when reading 'hands together'. Have a go at the following exercises – they are rather like a work-out for your brain. After playing through them, you should find the examples in this book quite straightforward. Come back to them whenever you feel like taking your brain to the gym!

In the first two exercises, play the upper line with your right hand and tap the rhythm with your left hand.

Now play the lower line with your left hand and tap the rhythm with your right hand.

Play the following two exercises while saying the words out loud – one word for each note. Maintain a steady pulse.

Play the upper line with your right hand and tap the rhythm with your left hand.

Play the lower line with your left hand and tap the rhythm with your right hand.

STAGE 2

Remember how important it is to *think in the key*. And to think in the key you must KNOW your key signatures!

Fill in the following table. It includes the new scales for Grade 2. If you know your key signatures it shouldn't take you very long.

The major key with no sharps or flats is _____ major

The minor key with no sharps or flats is _____ minor

The major key with 1 sharp is _____ major, and the sharp is _____

The minor key with 1 sharp is _____ minor, and the sharp is _____

The major key with 2 sharps is _____ major, and the sharps are _____

The major key with 3 sharps is _____ major, and the sharps are _____

The major key with 1 flat is _____ major, and the flat is _____

The minor key with 1 flat is _____ minor, and the flat is _____

If you made any mistakes, copy out this table and try again.

Before you begin each of the following exercises you need to say the name of the key. Then SAY each of the notes rhythmically and out loud. Don't play this set of exercises.

Play the notes in each of the following exercises in your own time. Think of each note's name before you play it. After you've played each exercise, make up your own tune using the same notes. As you play each exercise, remember to concentrate hard.

1 Before you begin, think A major = F♯, C♯ and G♯

2

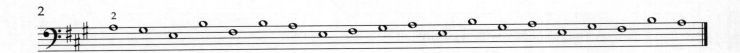

3

4

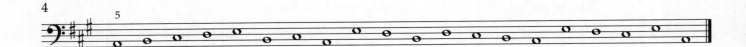

5 Before you begin, think E minor = F♯ and some C♯ and D♯ accidentals.

6

Follow the dynamic markings carefully in the next two pieces. Don't forget to *think in the key!*

7

8

STAGE 3

It's very important to have a good idea what a piece sounds like even before you play a single note! Sing a familiar or favourite song *silently* in your head (e.g. *Happy Birthday*, the National Anthem, etc.). You'll find that it's easy to 'hear' music in your head, just as you can with words.

Have a look at the next piece. Play the first note, and then try to imagine what the rest of the piece sounds like *in your head*.

Now play the whole piece. How close to the actual tune was your 'imagined' version?

Look at the next piece. Imagine what it sounds like in your head, then sing it at a comfortable pitch.

Now play it.

'Read' the next tune in your head. Do you recognise it? You'll soon be reading music just like you read words!

You might think that hearing two parts together in your head is really difficult. It's not! (Some people can hear a full symphony orchestra in this way.) 'Think' through *Happy Birthday* in your head – you will probably find that you're hearing the accompanying chords as well as the tune.

Try imagining both lines of the next piece in your head. Notice that both hands begin on Cs and then move to Gs half-way through bar 3.

Next, sing the upper line and play the left-hand line.

Now play both lines. How close was your imagined version?

Have a go at hearing each of these pieces in your head and then playing them in turn. How close were you each time?

Hear this piece in your head …

Now play it.

Hear this piece in your head…

Now play it.

Hear this piece in your head…

Now play it. How close were you?

STAGE 4

A major

RHYTHMIC EXERCISES

1

2

3

MELODIC EXERCISES

Play the following notes in your own time (see Introduction).

1

2

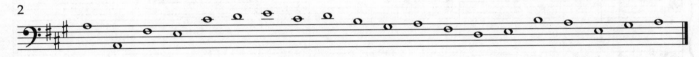

3 **Moderato**

4 **Allegretto**

4

PREPARED PIECE

Marks*

1 What will you count? Clap the right- then the left-hand part.

2 What key is this piece in?

3 Work out which fingers you will use on the first note of each hand and then write them in.

4 Which triads are formed by the notes in bar 6 (left hand) and bar 7 (right hand)?

5 Try to hear the piece through in your head. Now sing the right-hand part out loud while clapping the left-hand part.

6 Clap the first four bars of the left-hand part two or three times.
   Now try clapping them from memory.

Total:

Moderato

Unprepared tests page 25

Mark:

Prepared work total:

Unprepared:

Total:

*The mark boxes are to be filled in by your teacher.

STAGE 5

E minor

RHYTHMIC EXERCISES

MELODIC EXERCISES
Play the following notes in your own time (see Introduction).

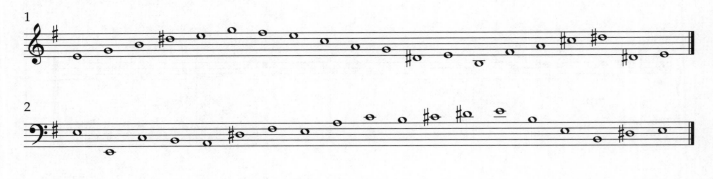

PREPARED PIECE

1 What will you count? Clap the right- then the left-hand part. ☐

2 What key is this piece in? What is the name of the second note in bar 1 (right hand)? ☐

3 How will the marking *Lento* affect your performance? What do **mp** and **mf** mean? ☐

4 Work out how you will finger the first bar of the right-hand part. Write the fingering in. How will you finger the final two notes of the right-hand part? ☐

5 Try to hear the piece through in your head. Now sing the left-hand part out loud while clapping the right-hand part. ☐

6 Clap the first four bars of the right-hand part two or three times. Now try clapping them from memory. ☐

Total: ☐

Unprepared tests page 26

Mark: ☐

Prepared work total: ☐

Unprepared: ☐

Total: ☐

Running totals:

4	5

STAGE 6

C major and A minor

RHYTHMIC EXERCISES

MELODIC EXERCISES
Play the following notes in your own time (see Introduction).

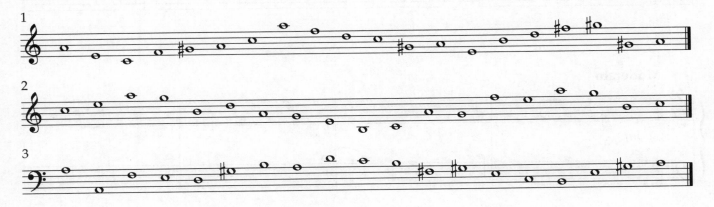

Andante

Alla valse

PREPARED PIECE

1 What will you count? Clap the right- then the left-hand part.

2 What key is this piece in? Play the scale. Have you learnt any pieces in this key?

3 What does *Allegretto* mean?

4 What rhythmic device is used in bars 1–2 and 3–4 (left hand)?

5 Try to hear the piece through in your head.
   Now sing the right-hand part out loud while clapping the left-hand part.

6 Clap bars 5–8 of the right-hand part two or three times.
   Now try clapping them from memory.

Total:

Allegretto

Unprepared tests page 27

Mark:

Prepared work total:

Unprepared:

Total:

Running totals:

4   5   6

STAGE 7

F major and D minor

RHYTHMIC EXERCISES

MELODIC EXERCISES
Play the following notes in your own time (see Introduction).

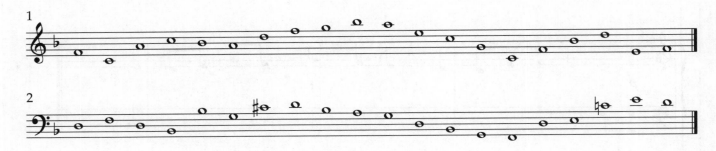

Allegretto

Cantabile

PREPARED PIECE

1   What will you count? Clap the right- then the left-hand part.

2   What key is this piece in? Play the scale and arpeggio.

3   What does *Andante* mean?

4   The notes in bar 2 (left hand) form part of which arpeggio?

5   Try to hear the piece through in your head. Now sing the right-hand part out loud
    while clapping the left-hand part.

6   Clap the first four bars of the right-hand part two or three times.
    Now try clapping them from memory.
    Look at the final four bars of the left-hand part for a few moments.
    Now try playing them from memory.

Total:

Unprepared tests page 28

Mark:

Prepared work total:

Unprepared:

Total:

Running totals:

4	5	6	7

STAGE 8

G and D majors

RHYTHMIC EXERCISES

MELODIC EXERCISES
Play the following notes in your own time (see Introduction).

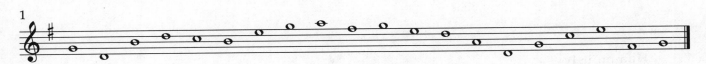

PREPARED PIECE

1   What will you count? Clap the right- then the left-hand part.

2   What key is this piece in? Play the scale and arpeggio.

3   Compare bars 1–2 (left hand) with bars 3–4 (right hand). What do you notice?

4   How would you describe the character of the music?
    How will you best achieve this in your performance?

5   Try to hear the piece through in your head.
    On a flat surface, tap the rhythm of both parts together.

6   Study the final four bars of the left-hand part for a moment.
    Now try playing them from memory.

Total:

Unprepared tests page 29

Mark:

Prepared work total:

Unprepared:

Total:

Running totals:

4	5	6	7	8

A SIGHT-READING CHECKLIST

Before you play a piece at sight always do the following:

1   Look at the time signature and decide how you will count the piece.

2   Look at the key signature and begin to *think in the key*.

3   Look at the tempo mark and any obvious technical difficulties and, taking both into account, decide what speed to play.

4   Scan through looking for the highest and lowest notes to decide which fingers you will use at the start of each phrase.

5   Notice any accidentals occurring during the piece.

6   Notice any scale and arpeggio patterns.

7   Work out leger-line notes if necessary.

8   Notice dynamic levels and other markings.

9   Decide what the character of the music is and how you will best achieve this.

10   Try to hear the piece through in your head.

11   Count at least one bar in (in your head) before you begin, to establish the pulse.

When performing your sight-reading piece, remember to:

1   Continue to count and think in the key throughout the piece.

2   Keep going at a steady and even tempo.

3   Ignore mistakes.

4   Look ahead – at least to the next note or beat.

5   Play expressively and try to give character to your performance; in other words, play *musically*.

6   **CONCENTRATE!**

UNPREPARED TESTS

Before you begin, go through the *Sight-reading Checklist*, page 24

STAGE 4

STAGE 5

STAGE 6

1 Allegretto

2 Andante

3 Flowing   rall.

4 Animato

5 Smooth blues (*swing the quavers*)

STAGE 7

STAGE 8

SUMMARY STAGE

More Improve your sight-reading!

The ability to sight-read fluently is an essential part of the pianist's training, not only as preparation for examinations but also as an accompanist or with an ensemble. Responding to demand, and building on the internationally successful series *Improve your sight-reading!*, Paul Harris has created a new supplementary series of sight-reading books. With further rhythmic and melodic exercises, prepared pieces and a variety of unprepared tests, these books will ensure that students gain the confidence they need in any sight-reading situation.

ISBN 0-571-52393-5 Piano Grade 1
ISBN 0-571-52394-3 Piano Grade 2
ISBN 0-571-52395-1 Piano Grade 3
ISBN 0-571-52396-X Piano Grade 4
ISBN 0-571-52397-8 Piano Grade 5

FABER *ff* MUSIC